THE DO-IT-YOURSELF GUIDE TO HARDWOOD FLOORING

Everything you need to know
to install, sand, and finish
hardwood flooring

by

Chip Alliman

A Complete
Do-It-Yourself Guide
to
Installing & Finishing
Hardwood Floors

■ Selection ■

■ Estimating ■

■ Budgeting ■

■ Tools & Supplies ■

■ Preparation ■

■ Installation ■

■ Sanding ■

■ Finishing ■

■ And more.... ■

CONTENTS

Introduction

Unfinished Hardwood Flooring

Hardwood flooring is one of the most important assets in any home. Not only do wood floors add value to your home from a financial point of view, they also add value in the overall warmth and appeal of your home.

In a survey of real estate agents across our country, 90 percent agreed that "houses with wood flooring sell faster and for higher prices than houses without wood floors."

The National Wood Flooring Association (NWFA) and the National Oak Flooring Manufacturers Association (NOFMA) have valuable websites for you to learn about the various hardwoods that are available today.

Wood floors are also becoming more popular because they are ecologically friendly. This renewable resource helps your home stay free of allergens to provide you with a health-friendly environment for your growing family.

Not only is cleaning and maintenance made easier with today's hardwood finishes, but hardwood is timeless and can last the life of your home.

This book is directed specifically at what is referred to as unfinished, site finished, or job site finished wood floors. You'll find an abundance of information on species, stability, hardness, and other important information about selecting the right hardwood for your home. More importantly, this book will help you better understand all of the processes involved in the installation and finishing of your hardwood flooring. We'll also give you information on the maintenance and care for the variety of wood floor finishes that are available today.

Hardwood flooring is like so many successful home projects in that it must begin with good planning and set up. The right species, the grain and color that will blend with other woods in your home, using quality stain and finish products, and a plan that helps you start the project right will pay off in the end result as carpet and other floor coverings have a more limited life span.

We urge you to read each chapter carefully and thoroughly, underlining and marking key points that will be applicable to your project.

We're assuming you are pretty handy and already have some of the basic tools required for general household repairs. Tools like pry bars, nail sets, and chalk lines are just a few of the hand tools necessary for hardwood flooring installation. In Chapter 4 we will give you a full list of the tools and supplies that you will need for this project.

Let's begin!

Chapter
1

Selecting the Right Hardwood

Above or Below Grade?

It is important to first determine the general areas where you will be installing the hardwood floors. In Chapter 3 we will help you create a complete budget.

Unfinished hardwood flooring is generally best suited for installation on wooden subfloors. The further you can keep hardwood from moisture, the better the stability.

If you are installing on the main floor of your home, for example, and you have a full basement or crawl space under the main floor then you are installing on grade or above grade. This means your hardwood will be equal to or above the level of the ground surrounding your home.

If you want to install hardwood on a level that is below grade, then you will normally be installing at a level that is below the level of the ground surrounding your home.

You'll need to do three things to protect your hardwood from the moisture the ground holds, especially during periods of rain and high humidity.

Below grade also means that your floor will be on some form of concrete. Concrete holds and retains moisture which can be very damaging to hardwood floors.

Although hardwood can be installed over concrete, in basements, or on ground level cement slabs, it requires that you consider an engineered wood that is generally available as a prefinished product that is constructed with layers of wood to help control shrinking and swelling. It may also be recommended that the engineered product be installed as a floating floor which means the floor is not connected to a subfloor and is free to expand and contract naturally. Generally, a layer of heavy plastic is installed over the concrete to help deflect moisture. Then a layer of sound proofing material, which is typically foam or cork is laid over this. Engineered wood is installed according to the manufacturer's guidelines. Newer products include click together systems, or sometimes flooring that is glued where the tongue and groove meet to keep the floor tight as it floats over the foam pad.

Solid hardwood floors are seldom recommended for below grade application. In those instances where it might be used there would be requirements of a subflooring installation prior to the hardwood being installed. For example, to install the standard 3/4 inch unfinished hardwood over cement we would always recommend that you first lay down a layer of heavy plastic, then two layers of 3/8 inch plywood floated over the entire floor. This is the only way to ensure that the moisture in the cement will not effect the stability of the hardwood. Using this method will also allow you to nail or staple the hardwood in place as you would in a normal installation.

Common Species

Selecting the correct type of hardwood is important as you consider the design elements of your overall home environment.

Although most homes have many species of wood in their furniture, cabinets, and interior trimwork, you should take into account the importance of blending with key elements of that wood.

For example, if you plan to install hardwood floors in the kitchen area and have red oak cabinets, then you must take into consideration that only those hardwoods that carry the red tones will blend nicely with your cabinets.

If you already have hardwood in some rooms and plan to add to what you have, you are generally advised to stay with the same species and grade. There are occasions when mixing species can be effective such as borders or insets. For example, if your home has white oak flooring in the entry, halls, and family room areas and you want to add the rectangular formal dining room, it can be effective to place a large border of walnut or santos mahogany with white oak in the central portion of the room. This sets the room off with a distinctive flair that can be warm and attractive.

The most commonly used hardwoods are:

    red oak
    white oak
    hickory
    walnut
    cherry
    maple
    brazilian cherry
    ash
    pine

For more information on species and grading go to the following websites:

    http://www.woodfloors.org/consumer/
    http://www.nofma.com/

Standard Widths

The most common width we see today is the 2-1/4" strip. In years past hardwood floors were made with strips as narrow as 1-1/2" which were attractive, functional, and stable. Hardwood cut in widths from 2-1/4" up to 4-3/4" is considered strip flooring. 5" and over is considered plank. The wider boards used today are more susceptible to expanding and contracting with the seasonal moisture adjustments. A wider plank has many more cells to take in moisture during the humid months, and many more cells to shrink in the dry season. Over time this will result in some minor cracks between boards. Most of us who work in the industry feel that cracks up to the width of a dime would be considered normal shrinkage in the dry seasons.

Wide Plank

Wide plank includes 5" and goes up to 7", 8", 9" and beyond. Again, the wider the plank the more seasonal movement you will see. It is not uncommon for hardwoods like southern yellow pine and even heart pine to be milled in widths up to 18 inches. Many homeowners who want to recreate the look of turn-of-the-century homes choose these wide, appealing boards.

Hardwood Stability

To give you insight regarding the stability comparisons of various hardwoods, the scale on the next page uses red oak as a base, or standard, to show how its stability relates to many other hardwoods when influenced by seasonal moisture fluctuations. All woods are hygroscopic and will expand as they absorb moisture and contract when the air around the wood is dryer than the wood itself. This is a natural effect in the material itself and cannot be changed. Each species reacts differently. For example a red oak floor which was correctly installed in the middle of the summer last year, is now showing some small cracks in January or February. This is due to the typical seasonal dryness in the winter along with an average central forced air heating system which dries the air as it operates, causing cracks that might measure 10/100 of an inch. In comparison, a mesquite floor of the same width under the same conditions and heating could likely measure up to 65% less than the 10/100 of an inch or .035/100 of an inch. Neither crack is unnatural or even unsightly. That is just the way wood normally reacts to the air around it.

Notice that the oaks are at the bottom of the scale below and are considered less stable. However, oaks have been a staple of the flooring industry for quite some time and are considered a very reliable and available product. If acclimated and installed according to industry standards any and all of the woods listed will provide you with a lifelong product.

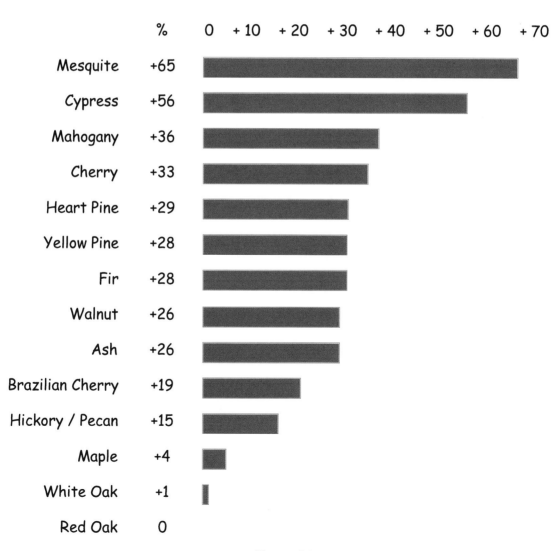

Hardwood Stability Comparison Scale
Based on the percentage of tangential shrinkage.

	%							
		0	+10	+20	+30	+40	+50	+60	+70
Mesquite	+65							
Cypress	+56							
Mahogany	+36							
Cherry	+33							
Heart Pine	+29							
Yellow Pine	+28							
Fir	+28							
Walnut	+26							
Ash	+26							
Brazilian Cherry	+19							
Hickory / Pecan	+15							
Maple	+4							
White Oak	+1							
Red Oak	0							

Stability Comparisons

White Oak	1%	more stable than red oak
Maple	4%	more stable than red oak
Hickory/Pecan	15%	more stable than red oak
Brazilian Cherry	19%	more stable than red oak
Ash	26%	more stable than red oak
Walnut	26%	more stable than red oak
Yellow Pine	28%	more stable than red oak
Cherry	33%	more stable than red oak

Hardness Comparisons

Walnut	22%	softer than red oak
Cherry	26%	softer than red oak
Yellow Pine	40%	softer than red oak
Ash	2%	harder than red oak
White Oak	5%	harder than red oak
Maple	12%	harder than red oak
Hickory/Pecan	41%	harder than red oak
Brazilian Cherry	82%	harder than red oak

Hard Or Soft?

The hardness scale on the following page is much like the stability scale as it compares the hardness factor of various hardwoods with each other.

The scale determines the hardness of wood in regard to the pressure it takes to dent a floor using the Janka hardness method. This is the measure of the amount of pressure in pounds that it takes to embed a .444" steel ball 1/2 of its diameter into the wood.

Hardwood Hardness Comparison Scale

**Ranked by the Janka Hardness Scale
for Wood Flooring Species**

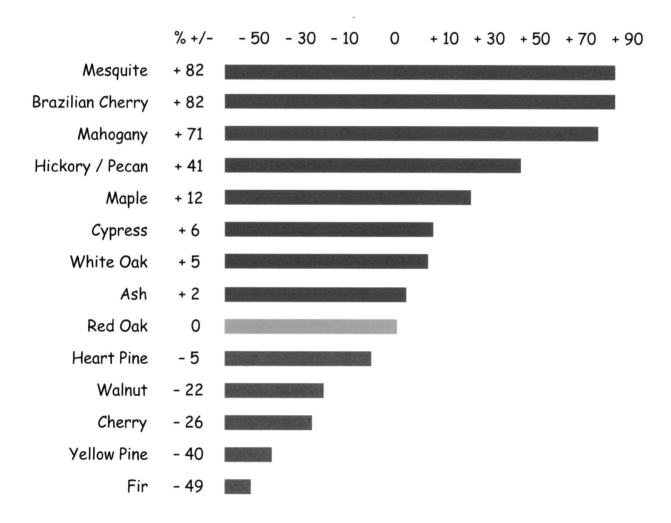

	% +/-	- 50	- 30	- 10	0	+ 10	+ 30	+ 50	+ 70	+ 90
Mesquite	+ 82									
Brazilian Cherry	+ 82									
Mahogany	+ 71									
Hickory / Pecan	+ 41									
Maple	+ 12									
Cypress	+ 6									
White Oak	+ 5									
Ash	+ 2									
Red Oak	0									
Heart Pine	- 5									
Walnut	- 22									
Cherry	- 26									
Yellow Pine	- 40									
Fir	- 49									

Different Grades Of Hardwood

Grading is a measure of several facets of the wood that relate to character, grain, and knots. All grades may come from the same tree and carry the same serviceable quality. Each grade is more about looks than usefulness or quality.

• Clear - (Not shown) Although with very close inspection some minor imperfections might be discovered, this grade is generally free of defects. You'll see Clear and Select used in many cabinet lines.

• Select - With some areas slightly lighter in color, this grade can have some slight imperfections in milling, a small tight knot every three feet or more, pinworm holes, and burls (rounded outgrowths). Darker areas referred to as "character," will usually not extend the entire length of the piece. Lengths will average longer in this grade, and you can find strips as long as eight feet.

#1 Common - In both #1 and #2 you will find more natural character in the knots and color variables. Generally knots in #1 will not exceed a half inch in diameter. Occasional grub worm holes and broken knots will be easily filled in the finishing process. Lengths vary, but a general average runs from two to six feet.

#2 Common - This grade is full of character and is used in homes where contrasting appearance and character marks are desired. Larger knots, more open and broken knots, and occasional pieces with broken tongue are admitted in this grade. There will also be numerous pieces referred to as "shorts" that average from nine to twenty-four inches in length.

#3 Common - (Not shown) This grade is very rustic in its general appearance with a great deal of color character and very large open knots.

Some sticker stain can be found in hardwood. Unfinished hardwood is stacked in bundles of approximately twenty square feet. The bands that hold the bundles together can leave marks from exposure to weather and sun. Most of these marks will sand out, but on occasion there can be deeper sticker stain. Heavier streaks of coloration, occasional machine burns, and a flag worm hole is also common.

Pricing runs parallel to the grades as listed above. Clear and Select

SELECT

#1 COMMON

#2 COMMON

OPEN KNOT

cost more per square foot than #2 Common, for example.

The photos on the previous page illustrate the variables in the grades. Although different mills might press the limits of grading, most mills, as members of National Wood Flooring Associations (NWFA) or the National Oak Flooring Manufacturer's Association (NOFMA) are required to grade by the industry grading rules. Our photos will give you an average look at the character differences of each.

The Effects of Stain

If you're leaning toward a very natural look in your hardwood floors, you might be pleased with applying just a sealer coat before the urethane finish. A natural or neutral sealer that is oil based will bring out the natural grains in the wood and help to richen the overall tone of the floor. An oil based sealer can be used even if you plan to use a water-based urethane for your finish. Let the sealer, or stain, dry well before the urethane is applied, usually 24 hours.

If a stain color is your choice, there are numerous stains on the market that will give you the depth, color, and tone that you desire. It is important to note that some hardwoods do not take stain well. Maple and hickory, for example, have dense areas in the wood which can prohibit the stain from soaking well into the wood. This can create a blotchy appearance depending on the darkness of the stain used. Lighter stains are recommended for some of the harder, more dense woods. In some cases, like maple, there are gel stains that can give you the consistency of color you desire. Call a woodworking shop in your area, to find out more about gel stains.

Climate and Hardwood Floors

The time of year and the weather in your area can influence when to install your hardwood flooring.

Wood soaks up moisture from the air, so if you're in the middle of hard rain storms in the spring or summer it would be wise to wait before you start your installation. The cells in the wood have taken in that moisture and are swollen, though you may not be able to see this. Installing now can result in some easily seen cracks in your flooring when that moisture dissipates and the wood shrinks back to its normal state. If you have access to a moisture meter, be sure your hardwood is reading within two points of your subfloor moisture level.

No matter what time of year you are installing it is always best to leave your hardwood in the areas for installation for a few days prior to starting your project. This lets the wood acclimate to its new environment. Remember, a one or two percent change in the wood's moisture content can make quite a difference when you spread that change across an entire room.

Do not bring your hardwood home and leave it on the floor of your garage until you're ready to install. Cement has moisture, and your hardwood will absorb that moisture very quickly.

Formulas for Random Widths

Random widths of hardwood have become very popular in remodels and new home construction. This is a process of using, for example, 2-1/4", 3-1/4", and 5" strips placed at random across the floor. Some prefer the uniformity of running the widths in order, then repeating the order. Others prefer to place the wood in a more random configuration. Either way, the 2-1/4" strip must run the full length of the installation, then the 3-1/4", etc.

The formula to purchase the wood for an installation like our example is quite easy to calculate. Let's assume you are installing a family room, kitchen, and entry. Your total square footage with waste is 500 square feet.

First add together the widths you will be using. In our example we add 2.25 plus 3.25 plus 5 for a total of 10.5. Next divide 2.25 by 10.5 for a total of .21 or 21%. So 21% of your wood will need to be 2-1/4" strip. Then we divide 3.25 by 10.5 and get .31 or 31%. Finally, we divide 5 by 10.5 and get .48 or 48%. Our totals should now combine for 100% (21 + 31 + 48 = 100).

So using those numbers we determine how much of each width we will need for our 500 square foot floor:

$$500 \times .21 = 105 \text{ sq.ft. of } 2\text{-}1/4"$$
$$500 \times .31 = 155 \text{ sq.ft. of } 3\text{-}1/4"$$
$$500 \times .48 = 240 \text{ sq.ft. of } 5"$$

From that calculation we have the numbers we need to order the wood:

$$105 + 155 + 240 = 500$$

Your local hardwood flooring dealer can double-check your figures to be safe.

A quick word on waste. On average, professionals add from five percent to ten percent as a waste factor in ordering the hardwood. If your rooms include angles, closets, and hallways you will need to use a higher waste factor.

To calculate a waste factor of 7-1/2% on the above example of a 500 sq.ft. floor we would take each of the square footage amounts and multiply that number by 1.075. For example, we calculated to need 240 sq.ft. of the 5" hardwood. Taking 240 x 1.075, we know we must order 258 sq.ft. to include the waste needed.

Kitchens, Baths, and Utility Rooms

Installing hardwood in kitchens, baths, and utility rooms can be stressful to many do-it-yourself homeowners. These are areas with a lot of water that can often spill or leak. Since water doesn't mix with any type of flooring we encourage you to take precautions before installing hardwood in those areas.

Every homeowner should have the name of a reliable plumber handy.

When it's time to reconnect the icemaker on the refrigerator, let a plumber do the job, and at the same time check the stability of your connections and water hose. When it's time to reset the stool in the powder room, let a plumber do the job. When you put in hardwood floors you are raising the flooring just enough that very often the stool will now require a double-wax seal. Only your plumber knows for sure.

✓ Selection Checklist

Areas to get hardwood:

_____   _____

_____   _____

_____   _____

_____   _____

_____   _____

_____   _____

Species we prefer:

_____

_____

_____

Width we like:

_____

_____

Grade to consider:

_____

_____

Stain colors to think about:

_____

_____

Chapter
2

Measuring and Estimating

Determining Square Footage

Once you have selected the species, grade, and finishes for your new hardwood floors, it's time to begin compiling your materials list for the project. The first step is to measure your rooms and areas and calculate the square footage of hardwood that you will need.

Nearly all unfinished hardwood will come in bundles that contain about twenty square feet. Bundle size is largely dictated by a mass that is not too heavy for handling and stacking purposes.

For our example on the next page we will generate our square footage and other materials based on a layout that includes an entry hallway, living room, dining room, kitchen, pantry, and family room. We have made the example areas in even square feet for simplicity. When you are doing actual measurements you are usually safe to round up to the nearest half foot or six-inch length.

We will also assume that all of the coverage area has a wood subfloor that will allow a standard nail or staple installation. We will also assume that the subfloor is level or near-level so there is no need for leveling the floor.

✓ Staining Checklist

❑ Stain

❑ Mixing stains

❑ Disposable rubber gloves

❑ Knee pads

❑ Quarter round

❑ Other trim

❑ Rags

❑ Towels

❑ Sweat band for forehead

Notes: _____

_____

_____

_____

_____

_____

_____

_____

_____

_____

_____

_____

For practical purposes, we will estimate on the basis that you have selected a #1 White Oak, 2-1/4 inch strip hardwood. You have also selected to stain the floor with a Nutmeg stain along with two coats of a water-based, semi-gloss, urethane finish.

Our layout below is not to scale, but it will give you a good idea of how square footage is measured and calculated. Let's do some measuring.

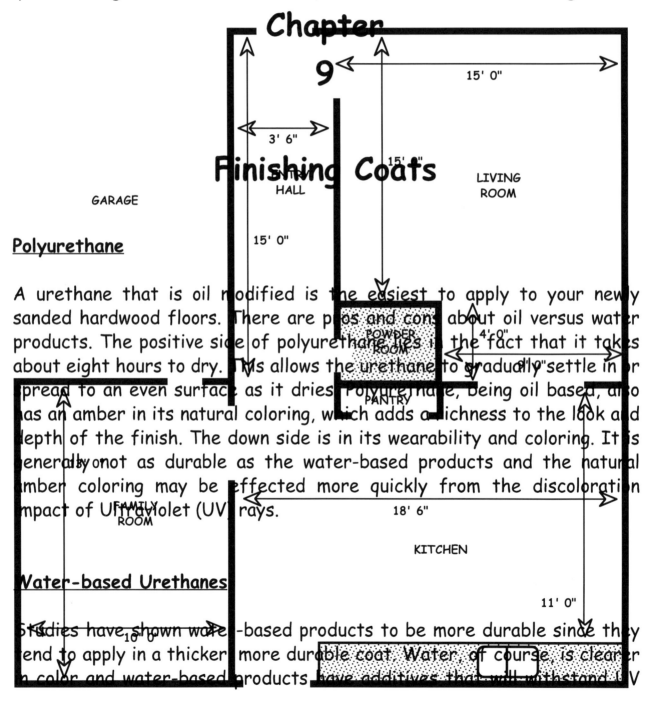

Polyurethane

A urethane that is oil modified is the easiest to apply to your newly sanded hardwood floors. There are pros and cons about oil versus water products. The positive side of polyurethane lies in the fact that it takes about eight hours to dry. This allows the urethane to gradually settle in or spread to an even surface as it dries. Polyurethane, being oil based, also has an amber in its natural coloring, which adds a richness to the look and depth of the finish. The down side is in its wearability and coloring. It is generally not as durable as the water-based products and the natural amber coloring may be effected more quickly from the discoloration impact of Ultraviolet (UV) rays.

Water-based Urethanes

Studies have shown water-based products to be more durable since they tend to apply in a thicker, more durable coat. Water, of course, is clearer in color and water-based products have additives that will withstand UV

Based on our model on the previous page, we list the measurements as follows. Note that 6 inches is one-half of a foot, therefore to multiply you use .5 for one-half.

Entry	3.5	x	15.0	=	52.5
Living Room	15.0	x	15.0	=	225.0
	9.0	x	4.0	=	36.0
Kitchen	18.5	x	11.0	=	203.5
Family Room	10.0	x	13.0	=	130.0
					‾‾‾‾‾
					647.0

Our project area is 647 square feet.

When ordering hardwood, it is important that you add about 5 percent to the total. It is very important to include a waste factor in your hardwood order since the end of many rows will leave you with cut-off ends that are not usable again. If you are very careful in your usage of the wood it can be done with a 5 per cent waste factor, but 7-1/2% is safe. It is always a good idea to have some hardwood remaining at the end of the project. A water leak, spilled chemical, or a dropped heavy tool can require some replacement at a future date and it is always good to have a small supply from the same mill run.

Using a waste factor formula of 7-1/2%, our final total of hardwood needed is:

$$647.0$$
$$\times \quad 1.075$$
$$\overline{}$$

Hardwood we need to order ---------   695.0   sq.ft.

This then is the amount of hardwood you need to order. There are several other items you will need to include in your materials order.

Nosing and Reducers

There might, for example, be a step down from the kitchen to the family room. If that is the case, you will need to install a piece of bullnose at the edge of that step down.

Nosing, or bullnose, must be installed before you get to that area so that you are careful to run the hardwood flooring flush to the full nosing.

Nosing is made to have a thicker end, or front, of the board that will overhang the step giving additional support to where you step as you leave or enter a room.

Nosing is also needed at the top of a stairway. If there is a rail around the stairwell, nosing should be used to overhang the stairwell and give a finished appearance from the stairway.

All nosing should be glued in addition to being top-nailed.

Reducers are used as transition strips from hardwood to another type of flooring. Since site-finished hardwood is $3/4$" thick it can require a transition to a vinyl floor, for example, which is normally $1/4$" thick to include the thickness of the vinyl's underlayment.

Professional hardwood flooring installers will often make a custom reducer for transitions. Many prefinished products have matching reducers available in lengths of about six feet, but most are pre-stained and finished, so you may have difficulty finding something that blends well with your floor color.

Quarter-round

Quarter-round is used at the base of cabinets in kitchens, baths, and utility rooms. Since there is usually a slight variation in the space where hardwood butts up to the bottom of a cabinet, installing a piece of quarter-round, stained and finished to match, will give you a finished look.

Quarter-round comes in a variety of widths and styles, but the more common products used in hardwood flooring are 1/2" x 1/2", 1/2" x 3/4", or 3/4" x 3/4". Choose a size that will compliment the cabinets, the amount of cabinet overhang, and the size of the room.

For a more finished look on corners and seams, it is best to cut the joining pieces at angles to help hide the joints. The photos on the following page will help you visualize those cuts.

Reducers can be made in a variety of sizes and styles. In most cases, there will be heavy foot traffic on your reducer, so don't make these large areas too thin. It is also very important that you glue your reducer in place. Nail it also, if you can nail it without causing the piece to split or crack. Small finish nails work best to hold the reducer snug while the glue is curing.

This is an end cut view of nosing installed at the top of a stairway. Notice that the portion of the nosing that is installed on the subfloor is 3/4" thick to be level with the hardwood flooring. The bullnose, which overhangs the edge of the subfloor, is 1-1/8" thick to allow for greater support on the edge that will carry the most weight.

Cutting an angle at a connecting joint will help hide the joint and give a more finished look.

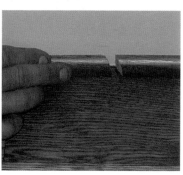

Cutting connecting corners at a 45-degree angle helps to give a rounded and finished look rather than a square open end.

✓ Measurement Checklist

Area	Width	x	Depth	=	Total
_____	_____	×	_____	=	_____
_____	_____	×	_____	=	_____
_____	_____	×	_____	=	_____
_____	_____	×	_____	=	_____
_____	_____	×	_____	=	_____
_____	_____	×	_____	=	_____
_____	_____	×	_____	=	_____
_____	_____	×	_____	=	_____
_____	_____	×	_____	=	_____
_____	_____	×	_____	=	_____
_____	_____	×	_____	=	_____
_____	_____	×	_____	=	_____
_____	_____	×	_____	=	_____
_____	_____	×	_____	=	_____

Total s.f. _____

Waste x 1.075

Hardwood I need to order _____

✓ Materials for Installation

Hardwood   Species   _____

                  Width   _____

                  Grade   _____

                  Square footage to order   _____

Nosing   Species   _____

                  Linear feet to order   _____

Reducer   Species   _____

                  Linear feet to order   _____

Quarter-round   Species   _____

                  Size   _____

                  Linear feet to order   _____

Chapter
3

Budgeting, Tools, and Supplies

Now that you have an idea of the materials you will need let's consider some of the products, tools, and supplies required to complete the project.

This chapter will help you develop a relatively complete budget that will list all of the items that you will need and formulate a total cost before you begin.

Before we plan a schedule and formulate a budget, you might consider those areas where outside help may be required. You may decide to hire a sub-contractor to perform some of the work. This can often prove more valuable than spending your own time and the cost of equipment rentals.

Although we will get into some of the specifics of removing and resetting stools and sinks in a later chapter, this is an area where you may want to call on an expert. Removing a sink or stool in a powder room is not overly difficult. You must be very careful not to bump and bang these heavy items since they can easily chip.

Resetting a stool can be a difficult project. Most often since the hardwood flooring sits higher than your previous flooring a double wax ring sealer must be used. Unless you are proficient with this, we encourage you to let a professional do this job. A leaky toilet will damage your new hardwood flooring.

On the following pages you'll see a list of various products, tools, and supplies you should have before you start your project. We have put a ballpark price beside some to help you toward a total budget figure. You may already have many of the tools so it won't be necessary to carry those prices out to the budget column.

✓ Budgeting

(BP represents Ballpark price)

Hardwood	Species, grade, width	
	_____	_____
Nosing	For stair tops and stairwells - BP about $4.00 linear foot	
	_____	_____
Quarter-round	For under cabinets - BP about $1.00 linear foot	
	_____	_____
Rosin or Felt paper	This is used as an underlayment to the hardwood to prevent squeaking. Comes in a roll of 100' x 4' to cover 400 s.f. - BP $20.00 per roll.	_____
Pry bar	_____	_____
Miter saw	_____	_____
Table saw	_____	_____
Jig saw	_____	_____
Floor nailer	- BP $35.00 rent per day	_____
Finish nailer	- BP $30.00 rent per day	_____
Flooring nails	_____	_____
Compressor/hose	_____	_____
Rubber hammer	_____	_____

Hammer _____ _____

Nail set _____ _____

12" Drywall trowel (To spread filler) _____ _____

Chalk line _____ _____

Glue   - BP $2.00 per tube

_____ _____

Belt Sander*   - BP $75.00 rental per day _____

Edger*   - BP $65.00 rental per day _____

Buffer*   - BP $65.00 rental per day _____

Filler   - BP $25.00 per gallon (400 sf)

_____ _____

Shop vac   - BP $35.00 per day

_____ _____

Stain or sealer   - BP $35.00 per gallon (500 sf)

_____ _____

Staining towels _____ _____

Paint brush _____ _____

Urethane   - BP $45.00 per gallon (500 sf)

_____ _____

Applicators   - BP $10.00 per coat

_____ _____

Other contractors _____ _____

* Plus the cost of abrasives

Chapter 4

Scheduling

Acclimation Time

It is very important that your hardwood be allowed to acclimate to its new environment before you install it. Ideally, you will place the hardwood in the rooms where it will be installed. Spreading the wood around the room is also helpful as it allows the flow of air to move in and around it.

The length of time for acclimation will vary depending on the area of the country you are in, the time of year, the altitude of your home, and other important factors that can effect hardwoods.

For example, if you live in Denver or Phoenix you are in dry climate. If your wood has been shipped from North Carolina you will want to be sure the wood has time to acclimate to your area.

If you are installing in the spring or summer and you have had several days of rain or higher than usual humidity, you'll want to give the hardwood additional time for acclimation. Allow the rain to stop, and the wood to fully acclimate.

Each area of the country will have different recommended acclimation periods so you are wise to check with your local dealer or distributor to be sure you are following their rules for hardwood in your area.

Remember hardwood takes on moisture and swells during rainy and moist seasons of the year. In the winter months, when your heat is on, that same hardwood will shrink as the cells dry. Don't be surprised when you have cracking in the dry seasons. You can find additional information on this characteristic at the NWFA and NOFMA websites (listed at the back of this book).

Prep Time

Prep time is how long you expect to spend removing the existing floor coverings, baseboard, and any other preparation that the floor will require before installation can begin.

The easiest way to remove carpet is with a sharp carpet knife. Cut the carpet across the room into strips about four feet wide by six to eight feet long. Roll these strips up, wrap them with twine, and dispose of them. Do the same with the carpet pad, although the pad is often secured with numerous staples that have to be plucked one-by-one. The tack strips around the edges also have to be pried up; make sure all nails are removed.

If you are removing old hardwood, disregard your desire to try and save it for future use. Many of the tongues and grooves will be split and destroyed in the removal process.

Vinyl or linoleum can be the most difficult floor covering to remove. It is important that you remove the vinyl but also the underlayment (if there is one) that was installed under the vinyl to assure a level and even surface. The difficulty comes in how it was originally installed. Often glues were used that can be very problematic to break free. On occasion a sander and heavy grit sanding belt are needed to remove some glues.

Removing baseboards can also be tedious depending on the age of the home, the size of the baseboard, how many times it has been painted and caulked, and other considerations. We'll have more on this in a later chapter.

The key to prep time is patience. The project is just beginning. Take your time in this important step. In planning your schedule allow more time than you might expect.

Installation Time

Installation time will vary depending on the tools you have or can rent, and your skill using those tools. Installation will also vary depending on the width of the hardwood you are installing. It will take less time to install 500 square feet of 5 inch, than it would to install the same square footage of 2-1/4".

Take time to lay out some rows, pound a row into the preceding nailed row, then run the nailer the length of the room being sure ends are tight. And cutting the last board in a row to run up to the wall will not go as quickly as you might have thought, especially the first time you do it.

Overall however, for planning and scheduling purposes, you can plan on installing from 200 to 300 square feet per day if the rooms are generally large and rectangular. If you are including hallways, closets, and angles - reduce that number by a fair percentage. And a helpful tim: do some stretch exercises before you start or your back will rise up in revenge the next morning.

Sanding Time

Sanding time is not as easy to project. Much of this time will depend on the quality of the equipment you have and your skill with that equipment.

Sanding time can also vary greatly based on the coarseness of the sandpaper belts and discs you use.

We recommend that you follow industry guidelines when it comes to this phase of the project since the floor will ultimately look only as good as your sanding patience and technique. For practical scheduling purposes you can almost parallel the time and square footage we noted in the previous Installation Time portion of this section. Safely plan on 200 to 400 square feet per day, again taking into consideration halls, closets, corners, and angles.

Finish Time

Stain time and finish coats can more easily be estimated since you must allow for dry time prior to the next phases or coat.

There are more specifics in Chapter 8 that might influence your scheduling, but you should count on a day to stain or seal, and one day for each urethane coat. As you will learn in Chapter 8, if your project is reasonably small and you are using a water-based urethane, it is possible to apply two coats in one day in some geographical areas.

Baseboard & Trim

Resetting baseboard is vital to the finished look of your project, so take your time, use proper equipment like a compressor and nail gun, and be sure to caulk for that finished look. We included some caulking tips in a later chapter.

Count on two to three hours per room or hall and closet area.

✓ Schedule Checklist

Acclimation time   _____ Hours   _____ Days   _____

Remove carpet/pad   _____ Hours   _____ Days   _____

Remove vinyl   _____ Hours   _____ Days   _____

Remove hardwood   _____ Hours   _____ Days   _____

Remove tile   _____ Hours   _____ Days   _____

Level floor   _____ Hours   _____ Days   _____

Remove baseboard   _____ Hours   _____ Days   _____

Install hardwood   _____ Hours   _____ Days   _____

Sanding   _____ Hours   _____ Days   _____

Edging   _____ Hours   _____ Days   _____

Stain or seal   _____ Hours   _____ Days   _____

First coat urethane   _____ Hours   _____ Days   _____

Second coat urethane   _____ Hours   _____ Days   _____

Reset baseboard   _____ Hours   _____ Days   _____

Total   _____

Chapter 5

Getting Started

Delivery of Hardwood

Since hardwood is heavy you will want to plan stack it somewhere in each room that is out of the way. We recommend you stack your hardwood in areas farthest from your starting line. For example, in the diagram on Page 20 you might place one-third in the family room outside wall and two-thirds along the living room outside wall. This will place the wood out of your way during most of your prep phase. Once you have run your starting line you will have good access to your wood without having it in your way.

Direction Of The Wood

Since it is always wise to do things according to the basic standards of an industry, this applies to the direction you run your hardwood. There are however, some considerations that you may choose to influence your decision in the matter.

The first rule is run your hardwood <u>across</u> the beams in the flooring. That is, determine which way the beams to which the subfloor is nailed run, and run your hardwood perpendicular to that. In newer homes the quality of modern subfloor materials is high enough that this is not always a tried and fast rule.

There is another, less stringent rule, and that is the appearance of your floor to the eye. It is always best, when you can, to run the hardwood the longest length of any room, hallway, or large entry. Optically, this gives the appearance of opening up the room rather than shutting the room off.

It is usually best not to mix the direction, although this can be done in certain circumstances. Sometimes a homeowner will want to run the hardwood at a 45 degree angle in a dining room with a 12 inch border around the entire room. This sets the room off from the rest of the hardwood and gives an appealing look. Generally, it is best not to run one room in one direction, then the hallway or an adjacent room in a perpendicular direction.

Your floor should compliment your home, and it does that best by being warm and inviting without drawing too much attention to itself.

Door Clearances

This is a critical phase and one that you must look at closely before you begin your project.

Using our floor plan on page 20 again, if the home was built years ago and vinyl or linoleum was used in the entry, kitchen and pantry areas there is a good possibility that the front door, rear door, and pantry doors are cut with a clearance that may be too low for hardwood. Often underlayment was not used when linoleum was installed. Even with a more modern vinyl floor with an appropriate underlayment it is likely that the total height of the flooring material above the subfloor is about $1/4$".

Since your new hardwood flooring will be $3/4$" in height, there is a possibility that some doors will have to be cut for proper clearance. This can present problems for an entry door with a fixed threshold. Take the time to measure and make sure the clearance is sufficient. If not, getting a referral for a good trim carpenter is something to consider.

Removing Stool and Pedestal Sink

As we mentioned in Chapter 3, removing a stool and/or pedestal sink in a powder room is heavy, but not too difficult. Once you have turned off the water it is a matter of disconnecting from the pipes and any wall attachment and lifting them out of their place. Be careful not to ding or bump them since they are easily chipped.

After more than two decades of experience in the hardwood flooring industry, this issue could be reduced to one sentence - "Call a plumber!" Removing a stool is much easier than reinstalling it properly once your new flooring is in place. If you're not an expert, don't risk this part of your project. Professional help can save you weeks of disappointment plus additional costs.

Removing Baseboard

Removing the baseboards is required before installation can begin. A utility knife, a wide chisel, a prybar, and a hammer should be all you need to remove baseboards in the project area. It is important that you run your new hardwood close to the wall at each end so the slightly staggered ends will be covered when you replace the baseboard.

Most baseboard has been installed with staples or finish nails and will pry off easily. Don't underestimate the importance of running a cut line at the top of the baseboard where it lays against the wall. Whether it was

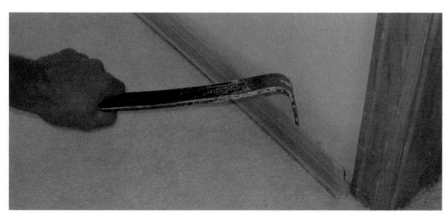

After running your knife along the top edge, a chisel is best to get the board loose and started. Then the short end of a pry bar works nicely as you waggle the bar right and left for pressure rather than up and down.

caulked, painted, or if there is wallpaper on the wall behind it, running that cut line will save you time and frustration. The cut line assures that when the baseboard is pried from the wall, it does not bring anything with it that is attached to the wall.

Carefully tap the chisel about an inch or so deep behind the baseboard at one end, then pry slowly to see if it will come loose easily. If it will, gradually work your way along that piece of baseboard until it is removed.

Warning: When you pry be careful that you don't let the chisel or pry bar have so much leverage that it sinks into the drywall behind the baseboard. This indentation will show later when you reset the baseboard. Often the best tool is a pry bar like you see in the photo below. As you can see, inserting the short end of the pry bar, then lightly moving it to the right or left (rather than up or down) will allow good leverage to loosen the baseboard.

Once the board is removed, be sure you number the back of that baseboard piece, putting the same number near the floor on the wall where you removed it.

This is also a good time to clean up your baseboard while it is stacked in the garage or basement. A new coat of paint will do wonders for scuffed baseboard and compliment your new flooring. If your baseboard is stained, find a stain that is close in color and, using a rag, wipe a new coat onto the baseboard. If you're really energetic you can brush on a coat of urethane too.

Removing Carpet

To repeat our comments under prep time in chapter 4, removing carpet will take time and labor. As we noted there the easiest way to remove carpet is with a sharp, carpet knife. Cut the carpet across the room into strips about four feet wide by six to eight feet long. Roll these strips up, wrap them with twine, and dispose of them. Do the same with the carpet pad, although it is often held in place with numerous staples that have to be pulled one-by-one. The tack strips around the edges also have to be pried up. Make certain all nails are removed.

Removing Tile, Vinyl, and Linoleum

In most cases tile, vinyl, and linoleum will have an underlayment under it. This is normally a sheet of plywood about 1/8" thick. It might be tacked or glued in.

It is important that you remove everything until you're down to the original subfloor. Stripping everything will assure you a level connection from one area to the next in your home without transition strips which can catch a toe or snag a sock.

In some older homes mastic glues were used to hold linoleum in place. These can be difficult to get up and may require a labor-intensive scraping of the area to get it to level and smooth. Doing a thorough job will pay dividends later.

Inspecting The Subfloor

Now is a good time to carefully inspect the subfloor. Walk it slowly looking for squeaks, nail heads, and loose or rotted boards. Often floors squeak because of the wood-on-wood where the subfloor is nailed to the beams below it. If this is the case drive a few deck screws into those boards to eliminate all movement.

Although you don't have to replace rotted boards, if the area is too large or too soft, you would be wise to replace them now.

Since you can't see under the subfloor, carefully nail or screw into the beams. There is always the possibility of a water pipe or electrical wiring running under the subfloor. It is wise to spend some time in your basement or crawl space looking for anything that could cause problems.

Check For Square

The next step is important. It will effect the finished look of your entire floor. If you are going to install the wood the length of the room rather than across the room, take a tape a measure from one side to the other at about three or four points in the room. You want to find out how consistent the room is in its width. If, for example, at one end of the room, the measurement is 10'2" and at the other end of the room 10'4" you will need to make some adjustments.

If you start installing on one side of the room using a straight line that is perfectly parallel to the wall on that side, then when you reach the final installation stage on the other side of the room your line is 2" off. This will become a difficult issue as you complete the install of the room.

By finding that variable at the beginning of your installation, you can start your flooring on a line that is visually acceptable to traffic areas, leaving a rear corner or wall of the room to help hide the discrepancy.

The Starting Line

Using our floor plan on page 20, we would recommend that you start your first row on the long wall adjacent to the garage. Let's assume again that you are installing 2-1/4" strip. Lay down a chalk line and start your first row about 2-3/4 inches out from the wall with the tongue of the wood facing away from the wall (This will leave a 1/2" space for expansion between your first board and the wall),

Putting the starting line 2-3/4" from the wall, place a mark at both ends. Pound in a finish nail at one end and slip the end of your chalk line over that nail. Stretch out the chalk line, making sure it is very tight with no obstructions, to the mark at the far end, and snap your starting line along the floor.

Since a floor nailer is powerful enough to slightly move a board when it drives in the nail or staple, it is certainly acceptable to facenail (topnail - see photo on page 51) the first row of boards to secure them before using your floor nailer. Be very careful that your first row stays right on our chalk line. If you start wrong, you'll finish wrong.

Rosin Paper

Now that we have our chalk line on the floor and your first row is in place it's a good time to roll out the rosin paper.

Roll the rosin paper the same direction as your starting row, working out from that row. Each row will need to overlap the preceding row by four to six inches. A few strips of masking or painters tape will hold the paper in place.

Note: The last row of paper should stop about twelve inches from the wall where you will finish. From that point on in, you will need to glue and top nail the hardwood rows in place since the floor nailer is limited in tight spaces.

Laying out your Bundles

Mills vary in the way they package and bundle their products. But typically your bundle will have three or four layers with tongues facing one direction and a top layer facing opposite and upside down to protect the wood surfaces. Be sure you lay your bundles out so the majority of the tongues are facing the same direction and the majority of the wood with its face surface to the top. This will become apparent when you open your first bundle. Then remove all straps and packaging and dispose of those items.

Setting up Shop

What we write in this section is meant to help you with better efficiency only; it is merely a suggestion. You may work more efficiently in a different way, you may be left handed and prefer a set up friendly to your habits, or this may be trivial to you.

Referring to our diagram on page 20, you will be installing the hall area first and making your end cuts in the kitchen. The chop saw should be set up in the kitchen near the counter. Try to keep your compressor near the middle of your work area and behind you, so you can run up and down rows without having to maneuver the hose around obstacles. The table saw would normally be set up outside or in the garage area for its limited use.

Setting your chop saw at the end of your working rows and behind you will give you immediate access where you need it. Placing the table saw at the opposite end keeps it close by but out of the way. The table saw is needed to rip boards as you start and run up to the walls, or in instances where you must go around an island, fireplace, or other obstacle on the floor.

Laying out your your hardwood in front of you all the way down the line gives you easy access to a variety of lengths that will be needed to avoid the "H" or stair step patterns noted on page 46. Even with careful racking you will come across an occasional board that is warped or damaged. Having plenty to draw from makes it easier to keep moving down a row.

Properly installed hardwood has a blend effect that allows the eye to see the warmth and beauty of the entire landscape rather than be pulled to a specific pattern distraction.

✓ Startup & Setup Checklist

❏ Door clearances   Notes: _____

                                                  _____

❏ Direction of wood _____

❏ Remove stool _____

❏ Remove pedestal sink _____

❏ Remove baseboard _____

❏ Remove old flooring _____

❏ Inspect the subfloor _____

❏ Check for square _____

                                                  _____

❏ Starting line _____

❏ Rosin paper _____

❏ Laying out bundles _____

❏ Setting up your tools _____

                                                  _____

Chapter 6

Installing

Using the Nailer

There are two kinds of flooring nailers. One is pneumatic, which means it is powered by an air compressor. The other is manual, which means you power it. Use this tool all day for a month and you'll be pitching for the Yankees. The more commonly used is the pneumatic floor nailer.

If you're installing standard ³/₄" strip hardwood, load the nailer with

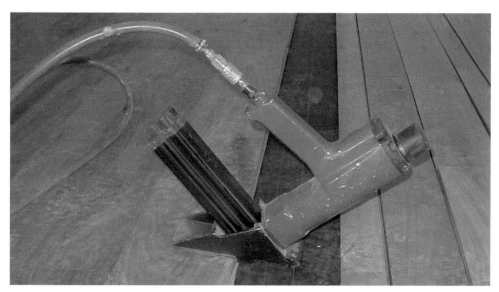

The pneumatic nailer shown here is like the manual nailer that can be used, except for the hose connector on the pneumatic nailer. Both will give you the same nail angle. The difference is in the pressure you must apply to drive the nail. The pneumatic only takes a light tap, the manual takes a moderate to full swing of your arm.

2" flooring nails. If you were shooting the nails straight down into the board you wouldn't use such a long nail, but since the flooring nailer shoots the nail at a substantial angle the 2" nail will give the floor good stability.

If you are installing over a wood subfloor that has pipes or radiant heat of some kind that is attached to beams under the subfloor and up tight against that subfloor, you will want to use a shorter nail.

It is important to test your nailer before starting your installation. To do this, connect your hose to the nailer and the compressor, and start the compressor to build pressure. There are adjustment knobs on the compressor that will let you control how high you want your pressure to build and rebuild during the installing process. Generally about 100-plus pounds is sufficient.

In the photo below, you can see the pressure to the nail gun has been set to maintain at about 85 lbs. This needs to be set at a number that will drive the nail into the board far enough to be slightly below the surface of the board. If the nail head is not deep enough, the tongue and groove will not fit snugly on your next board. On the other hand, you don't want the nail to be countersunk so deeply that it splits the tongue. This adjustment can vary depending on the nailer and the species of hardwood, but you might start at about 80 pounds as you test the nailer.

The photo on the next page shows you how to set the nailer against the tongue side of the board, allowing the edge across the bottom of the nailer to fit snugly in the groove above the tongue. This allows the nail to shoot into the board at the top of the tongue and down through the tongue and into the subfloor at the desired angle.

Compressor pressure guage and Nail drive pressure guage

Notice how the 1/4" edge along the bottom of the nailer fits snugly into the groove above the tongue. This directs the nail through the top of the tongue at an angle to give the floor the stability it will need.

That Critical First Row

Refer back to "The Starting Line" in chapter 5 to review the importance of laying out the first row. Just as a good carpenter measures twice and cuts once, we recommend you read that section again. This is one of the most important parts of your project. Time spent here will save a good deal of time and frustration later.

Remember as you start a row against one wall, the tongue should face the large open area of the room. This will be the direction you will be moving. As you start your rows near this wall, leave $1/2$ to $3/4$ of an inch to give the wood room for its seasonal expansion. This gap needs to be covered by your baseboard or quarter-round, so be certain you don't leave more gap than your trim will cover.

Ending The Rows

As a practical tip, set in a complete row before nailing. Then pick up your floor nailer and work your way down the same row, nailing about every eight to twelve inches along that row. When you come to the end of each row, it will require that you cut a board to end the row. A nice shortcut to measuring for this is to spin the end board around and mark it where it meets the end of the previous board. See the following photo and notice how the board is turned for marking. This mark tells you exactly where to

By turning the last board in a row so the groove faces the wall, you can mark where you want to cut the board with your chop saw. When you connect the board at the end tongue and groove, the cut end of the board is against the endinging wall.

cut the board so that it will fit the space left in the row up to the ending wall.

Here is another tip: If the remainder of the board you just cut to finish the row at the ending wall is long enough, it can be used to start the next row at the starting wall since the end that is cut will go under your baseboard and on the other end you still have a tongue.

Random Widths

We talked about random widths in chapter 1. If this is what you plan to do racking is very important. Random width means *random*. <u>Do not</u> run a row of 2-1/4, then 3-1/4, then 5" - only to repeat the same pattern in the next three rows. You might run a row of 2-1/4, then 5, then 3-1/4, then 5 again, then 2-1/4, etc. Mix it up, but take the time to plan ahead as you go, so you end up with a truly random look. The photo gives you a good example of a random width floor.

Random width installation must be truly random. Plan ahead so you don't end up with something that looks more like a formula rather than random. Remember also that when the floor is complete, there will always be much more of the wider plank than the more narrow boards. The boards need to blend together and not looked staged.

You can immediately notice an "H" (left). Several of them in the floor become distracting. Also note the stair step effect (right) that can also distract the eye.

When you cut off the end of your glue tube, cut it off at about the first cut mark so the opening is large enough to give you a bead of less than a quarter inch.

Shoot the top nails straight down into the board to hold all edges until the glue sets.

Watch Those Ends and Avoid Those H's

There are standards in the hardwood flooring industry that are wise to adhere to, so in laying out our flooring we select certain lengths of boards to run along previous rows making sure we stay in accord with those standards.

For example, in the first picture following we see what is called an "H." We <u>do not</u> want H's. We don't want anything to call attention to the floor. Any sort of pattern will catch the eye.

Another thing to avoid is close end joints. Keep your end joints at least 6 inches from each other. This will also help avoid squeaks.

As you lay down a board, be sure you fully insert the groove onto the tongue of the previous board. Double check to avoid the H. Use the rubber end of your installing hammer to bang the side of the board until it is fully up against the previous row. Then tap the open end of the new board to be sure the tongue and groove ends are tight.

Gluing and Topnailing

As you work your way across your floor, you will encounter obstacles. It is important to know the most practical and stable way to glue and topnail those rows where you are too close to get your flooring nailer to nail at the right angle. Normally this will include several rows of hardwood.

First lay out a bead of glue. We use a standard subfloor adhesive. Don't make the bead too thick, but wide enough to spread under the ends and center portions of all the boards you will be installing.

Set a row from start to finish. Then, using your finish nailer shoot a series of $1\text{-}1/2$" nails into the top of the board. Two top nails about every eighteen inches will suffice since the glue will give the boards the stability they need. The nails are only meant to hold the row in place while the glue sets.

Make sure the top nails have enough pressure to counter-sink their heads. In the sanding phase filler will cover these small holes.

Finally, when you install the last row or two next to an obstacle, use your pry bar to pull the boards tight to the preceding row before nailing. You might review the pry bar method used in the Removing Baseboard section in chapter 5.

Thresholds, Doors, Vents, Outlets

As you encounter other obstacles in your installation project, you will need other hand tools. For example, you will want to keep your jig saw near your table saw. The table saw gives you a nice table to lay or clamp a board as you make cuts for around door jambs, floor vents, floor electrical outlets, fixed thresholds, and other obstacles in your floor.

Putting a new blade in your jig saw will make the job easier. The species of wood you are installing will dictate, to some degree, how fine-toothed the blade should be for easy and accurate cutting.

✓ Installation Checklist

❏ Floor nailer   Notes: _____

❏ Finish nailer   _____

❏ Chop saw   _____

❏ Table saw   _____

❏ Jig saw   _____

❏ Rubber-end hammer   _____

❏ Nail puller   _____

❏ Pry bar   _____

❏ Glue   _____

❏ Compressor and Hose   _____

❏ Organizing your tools   _____

❏ Charge compressor   _____

❏ Set nail drive pressure   _____

❏ Measure first row - twice   _____

❏ Lay down the starting line   _____

Chapter

7

Sanding

<u>Belt Sander</u>

The belt sander is the workhorse for this phase of your project. This tool requires both brute force and a soft touch. The most commonly used

The belt sander takes a soft touch to achieve an evenly sanded floor. Note the belt that the worker wears that snaps on to the handle to give more leverage when he pulls back down the floor against the pull of the sanding belt.

sander is the belt sander. Anything less than a belt sander probably **won't** have the aggressive capability to properly sand your new hardwood flooring. Be sure you follow all of the safety instructions that come with any sanding equipment.

We go into more detail about the grit of the sanding belts you will need in a later section of this chapter. Be sure someone at your rental company goes over the operation of the sander to familiarize you with its use. There are numerous cautions that you must exercise in using this powerful tool. For example, <u>always go with the grain of the wood</u> and never across the grain. Run the length of the boards. Crossing the boards will leave sanding marks that will be visible in the final finish. Once you are ready to begin sanding you must release the drum to the floor slowly and gently as you allow the sander to pull you forward. Think of the process like an airplane taking off and landing. The sander must be moving when the drum makes contact with the hardwood. A quick drop of the drum will put a nasty rounded indentation in your floor that is not easy to remove. Warning: If you do put one of those belt indentations in the floor, gradually sand it out the best you can. As the wheels of your sander go over an indentation like that, they automatically put another indentation in the floor. Each time the drum touches the floor it creates one more indentation. This is called "chatter" and the finished floor, in the certain light, will look like a roller coaster.

Another caution comes when you reach the forward end of the floor. You are moving toward the wall slowly, so you will again gradually pull the drum off the floor to move to the next section, careful to not stop before the drum is off the floor. If you are using an eight-inch belt sander, it is best on the first sanding to overlap your sanding cuts about fifty per cent. So make your eight-inch cut, then pull back on the same line. When you start forward for your second cut, overlap your original cut about fifty per cent.

Using the belt sander in one sense is easy. In another sense it is very delicate. A sanded floor is like a painted wall. Every mark or bump that you thought the finish would cover stands out like a searchlight on a dark night. There is no need to get too close to the walls. You will use an edger for that portion of the floor.

The grit you will need for your sanding belts and edger discs can vary, depending on the species of wood you are finishing. For standard oak flooring the following would be a good example to follow for grit usage as well as the order of your sanding and procedure through the stain or sealer process. The following assumes renting a 110 volt drum, or belt, sander:

First sanding belt and edger disc	50 grit
Buffer sanding disc	50 grit
Apply filler	Filler
Second sanding belt and edger disc	80 grit
Scrape or hand sand corners	80 grit
Buffer sanding screen	80 grit
Vacuum	Not once - twice
Stain or seal	

Edger

Edgers are delicate sanding machines. Since they rotate, you will always be going across grain to some degree. Again, one of the keys to all sanding is to keep moving. Although you move the edger out and back, right and

Use the edger to sand with the grain as much as possible. Note the highlighted area where the abrasive is actually doing the cutting.

left, you must always be sensitive to the potential for swirl marks. These are often difficult to see until you apply stain and finishes, so you want to look closely as you use this sander. The edger is a machine that you must feel your way through more than think your way through. The weight of the edger is enough to do the sanding without any further downward pressure. In fact, as you feel your way along a wall area you will find that you don't let the full weight of the tool do the sanding. It will be your partial release of it's weight that will do the delicate work. You would be wise to do a practice run in an out-of-the-way area first.

This photo shows how you will need to turn the edger to make a smooth cut against walls and obstacles, and at corners.

Buffer

At some point in your life you have probably run a buffer. Whether it was in basic training in the military or a school job, you know the basics of buffing. When you lift the handle slightly the machine goes one way, when you let it down slightly it goes the other direction.

Start in an open area until you get the feel of the buffer. Screening the floor will give it the smooth final finish that you need before staining. Go slow and above all, be careful next to walls, cabinets, stair rails, or other obstacles. The purpose of the buffer is to help you blend the edges and body of the floor where different methods of sanding were used. A buffer is essential to a professional looking result.

Hand Sander

A small orbital hand sander will be necessary to get into areas where the belt and the edger will not go. Pantries, small closets, and corners will be much easier with a hand sander. A small sander will also help you correct other sander marks that have been left in the floor. It also forces you down on your knees where you will more readily see any of those marks. Remember: once you stain, there is no going back. Make sure your floor is well sanded.

Scrapers and Sanding Blocks

A small, sharp, metal paint scraper will make getting all the way into corners much easier. Be sure you always scrape with the grain of the wood to limit deep gouges or scratches. After some scraping it is always good to use a sanding block or orbital sander to remove surface scratches left by the scraper and also to blend the area with the adjacent surface.

Grit Matters

Following appropriate grit guidelines can save you from headaches down the road in your finish process. Even the color of your stain can be changed by using a more course grit on your final sanding. As you move through your various grits, not only are you taking out previous sander marks and minor swirls, but you are slightly closing the grain of the wood. This will effect the amount and depth of the stain application. The higher the grit on the final sand, the more the stain will stay on top of the wood, leaving it lighter in overall depth and color. See your stain manufacturer guidelines for the final grit recommended.

Full-trowel Filler

Filler is used to fill small cracks on the floor, especially near the end of boards. As a board comes off the production milling line it can sometimes move slightly to the right or left leaving a small variation in the edge of that board. These cracks, along with open knots if you are using a lower grade hardwood, should be filled to give a solid surface prior to urethane coats. It would be wise to include a large bucket of filler in your materials purchase. Using a twelve-inch putty knife you literally trowel the filler over the entire floor so all cracks and small blemishes get filled - even the ones you can't easily see. Let the filler dry for the recommended time. Filler will also help help you see imperfections in the sanding job and allow you to correct those areas in your final sanding.

A Final Sand

A final sand with an 80 grit belt sander and edger will serve as your final sanding and preparation. Again, keep your eyes open for swirls and other imperfections.

Screen For Best Results

After a quick surface vacuum to suck up filler dust from the final sanding, a buffer and an 80 grit screen will get your floor flat and smooth. Take your time here. You're creating your final product. Be careful not to leave any marks on the floor at this stage. Heavy boots and other footwear can leave marks on the raw floor. Now is not the time to risk that. If necessary, take off your boots or heavy shoes to keep the beautiful appearance that you have created through your hard work mar free.

Vacuum, then Vacuum Again

And vacuum another time. Nothing we can say will stress how important this phase is to the ultimate quality of your floor's finish. It is impossible to not have a tiny amount of dust in your floor's finish since there is dust in the air and some will settle in your finish no matter how careful you are. Even the smallest dust particle will leave a small spec in your finish. Don't be alarmed when that occurs. Many of these tiny bubbles or specs will walk off over time. Whatever steps you take to minimize these will be rewarded when the project is complete. We suggest you vacuum using an end piece with bristles or felt. This will help you to not leave marks from the plastic or metal edges on many vacuums. Remember that even a drop of sweat will leave a mark at this stage of your flooring process. Care must be taken here to assure a beautiful flooring finish.

✓ Sanding Checklist

❑ Belt sander

❑ Sanding belts

❑ Edger

❑ Edger belts

❑ Filler

❑ Orbital sander

❑ Scraper

❑ Sanding block

❑ Buffer

❑ Buffer abrasives

❑ Vacuum

Notes: _____

_____

_____

_____

_____

_____

_____

_____

_____

_____

_____

_____

_____

Chapter 8

Staining or Sealing

Sealing Is Natural

It is important that you apply a sealer coat to your hardwood before you apply a urethane finish. The sealer will seal the pores so that the urethane will stay on top, where it can protect the hardwood. NOTE: Nearly all stains contain a sealing agent. If you are looking for a lighter, more natural appearance for your hardwood, your process should include one coat of a natural or neutral sealer, followed by two or three coats of urethane.

In Chapter 9 we will discuss the differences between oil-based and water-based products. If you decide to use a water-based urethane it is still possible to use an oil-based stain or sealer. The advantage of the oil-base is to bring out the grain of the wood and give the floor a richer, warmer look. The application of a water-based urethane over the oil-based stain or sealer is all right if you allow the stain or sealer to dry completely in accordance with the manufacturer's instructions. It is also acceptable to put an oil-based urethane over a water-based stain or sealer, however sandwiching oil and water (oil-water-oil, or water-oil-water) can lead to problems.

Mixing Stains

Many people mix stains to better reflect the exact color they desire. Never mix oil-based with water-based stains. It is advisable to stay with the same manufacturer when mixing stains and to be very careful to measure the amounts of stain colors that make up your mix and record them for future reference. Keep some extra stain mix for possible future repairs.

Caution on the Use of Darker Colors

Dark stains can be more difficult to apply since they have greater tendencies to show overlap areas or areas of inconsistency if the application gets sloppy. Dark stains will also show sander marks more readily. Be careful if you decide to use these.

Staining

The most practical way to stain a floor is to wear knee pads, gather several paint rags or towels, and pour some stain on an area where you want to begin. You'll want about a 12 inch circle of stain. Use one of your towels to work the stain into the floor. It won't take a lot of pressure, just work it in and keep moving.

Working your way along an area that is about six feet wide by three feet deep use up the puddle of stain that you poured. Now take a clean towel or heavy rag and go back over the same area wiping up the excess stain and working the stain into the hardwood. Move your rag or towel with the grain as much as possible. Move on to the next area. Once you begin the staining process, keep going until you are finished. Stopping creates overlaps.

Be careful of your knee pads. If you happen to get too close to the stain and get it on your knee pads, you'll leave imprints that can show up in the final finish. It is good to wear throw-away rubber or vinyl gloves also, but again be careful where you place your hand if it has stain on it or you'll leave a hand print.

Avoiding Overlap Marks

If you start at one point on your floor, then end back at that same point an hour later you will have overlap marks where you started unless you plan your route. In our floorplan on page 20 we would begin with the kitchen / living room exterior wall moving across the floor in six-foot wide strips, moving with the grain. Complete the full six-foot strip in both rooms, then move left to the next six-foot strip ultimately ending in the hall area at the door to the family room. Start next on the far side of the family room, moving back toward the door and eventually exiting the area through the garage door. This will help you move across the floor without without having to blend with an area that has begun to dry.

Staining the Quarter Round

While your can of stain is open and before you install your trim, apply and wipe down your quarter round or any trim pieces that you will be using. Pour some stain into a small container, coffee can, or glass jar. Dip a corner of a small piece of rag or towel and dab it along the length of the quarter round. Leave it for only a moment, then wipe it well with a clean rag or towel.

Water Spots and Dry Time

Although you could walk on the floor an hour or two after staining, be sure to do it in slippers, socks, or footwear that will not mark the newly-stained floor.

Stain does not mix with water, so be especially careful not to splash even a drop of water on your newly-stained floor. Water, by morning, will turn that spot a different color.

This applies to sweat drops as well. As you are staining or coating your floor, wrap a towel handy to wipe off sweat before it beads and drops onto the stain or finish.

✓ Staining Checklist

☐ Stain

☐ Mixing stains

☐ Disposable rubber gloves

☐ Knee pads

☐ Quarter round

☐ Other trim

☐ Rags

☐ Towels

☐ Sweat band for forehead

Chapter

2

_____

_____

Measuring and Estimating

_____

Determining Square Footage

_____

Once you have selected the species, grade, and finishes for your new hardwood floors, it's time to begin compiling your materials list for the project. The first step is to measure your rooms and areas and calculate the square footage of hardwood that you will need.

Nearly all unfinished hardwood will come in bundles that contain about twenty square feet. Bundle size is largely dictated by a mass that is not too heavy for handling and stacking purposes. _____

For our example on the next page we will generate our square footage and other materials based on a layout that includes an entry hallway, living room, dining room, kitchen, pantry, and family room. We have made the example areas in even square feet for simplicity. When you are doing actual measurements you are usually safe to round up to the nearest half foot or six-inch length. _____

We will also assume that all of the coverage area has a wood subfloor that will allow a standard nail or staple installation. We will also assume that the subfloor is level or near-level so there is no need for leveling the floor.

For practical purposes, we will estimate on the basis that you have selected a #1 White Oak, 2-1/4 inch strip hardwood. You have also selected to stain the floor with a Nutmeg stain along with two coats of a water-based, semi-gloss, urethane finish.

Our layout below is not to scale, but it will give you a good idea of how square footage is measured and calculated. Let's do some measuring.

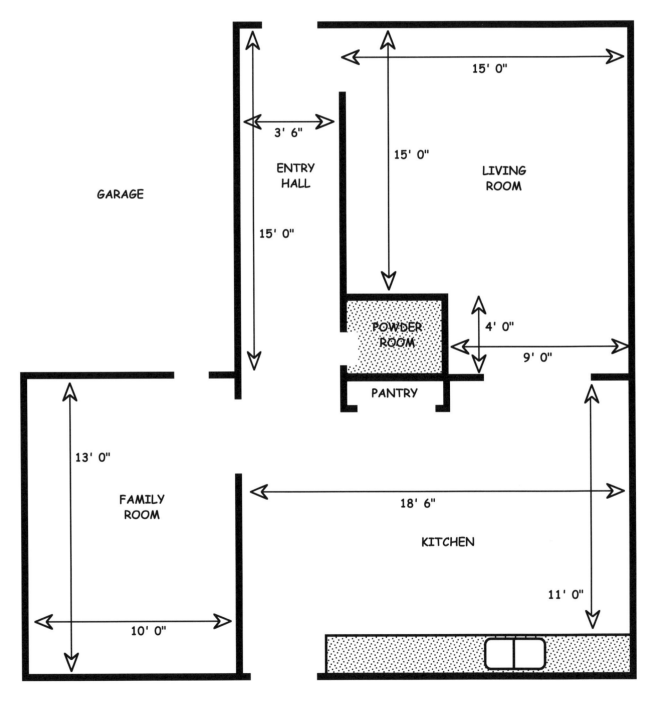

Chapter
9

Finishing Coats

Polyurethane

A urethane that is oil modified is the easiest to apply to your newly sanded hardwood floors. There are pros and cons about oil versus water products. The positive side of polyurethane lies in the fact that it takes about eight hours to dry. This allows the urethane to gradually settle in or spread to an even surface as it dries. Polyurethane, being oil based, also has an amber in its natural coloring, which adds a richness to the look and depth of the finish. The down side is in its wearability and coloring. It is generally not as durable as the water-based products and the natural amber coloring may be effected more quickly from the discoloration impact of Ultraviolet (UV) rays.

Water-based Urethanes

Studies have shown water-based products to be more durable since they tend to apply in a thicker, more durable coat. Water, of course, is clearer in color and water-based products have additives that will withstand UV rays and normal discoloration. UV rays tend to discolor wood itself in the form of a bleaching effect, so all products will discolor over time.

Many families have members who deal with allergies, sinus issues, and other needs to avoid contact with the odors and chemicals in polyurethane. Water-based products have a very mild odor and dry in less than three hours, which makes them very practical for these situations.

Applicators

It is important to use the correct applicators when you apply the finish to your new floor.

The most common applicators for polyurethane are the lambs wool flat applicators. The lambs wool slides onto a wood block that connects to a screw in broom handle.

The applicator often used to apply water-based products looks similar to a small paint roller with a very closely-cropped, fuzzy-looking surface.

In the application of either product the procedure is to follow the same general sequence as with your stain coat, starting along the far wall in our floor plan example on page 22.

Begin by using a brush for your edges, working out from the wall

Lambs wool applicators are more commonly used with oil-based finishes.

Water-based applicators look like a fuzzy paint roller but work well with the slightly thicker finish.

approximately six inches. Edge only that part of the wall in the area where you are working.

Next, pour a small amount in a puddle on the area where you have begun. Spread the urethane over an area about six feet out from the wall with your applicator. As you spread it, follow the grain of the wood and apply pressure to make the application even and well thinned. It is always best to use long, smooth strokes being careful not to leave overlaps. Use the applicator like the sander with an airplane takeoff and landing motion. Abrupt stops will leave marks and puddles. The goal is to build two or three thin coats. Each manufacturer will give you guidelines for coverage.

No Debris

No matter what applicator you use and regardless of how careful you were in vacuuming, there will still be dust and even some very small debris that you will pick up as your work your way across the floor. Stop occasionally and check for this on your applicator. Clean it as quickly and carefully as you can to be sure the dust and debris does not get worked into the finish.

As you move along the floor, watch for very small pieces of debris or tiny dust balls. You may not see them all as you work across the floor, but they will be easily seen in the dried finish. Remove them at once, being careful not to leave footsteps in the wet finish.

Use Your Daylight

It is always best to apply urethane in the daylight, allowing as much light as possible into the work area. Since even professionals can sometimes have an overlap line, natural light is helpful to identify flaws in your finish while there is still time to fix them. Watch for tiny debris as you go along. Occasionally an area of a board will soak up the urethane completely, and as you look back it will appear as a dry spot or a small area that appears to have been missed. You can avoid going back on the first coat since the second coat will cover that area. But on the final coat, if possible to reach that area, rework it a little to be sure the dull spot is worked out. Fix it now. It will be even more apparent when all the finish coats have dried.

Make an Exit Plan

By referring back to page 20, our sample floor plan, you can see that the rooms circle the powder room and pantry area in the center of the home. It is important that you have a plan of action before you begin since it is possible that if you start in the wrong area, by the time you work your way around the circle the urethane is setting up and you will certainly have overlap marks where the finishes meet. Plan now to stop at a threshold area, where wood runs across a doorway. An exit plan is even more critical when working with water-based products that set up quickly and dry in much shorter periods of time.

Shut Down Air Movement

Since there's always dust in the air, there are small particles of dust on your walls, window coverings, light fixtures, and other fixed objects in your home. Before you put a new coat of stain or finish on your floor, close all windows and doors to other parts of the home, turn off all fans and, if possible, turn off, or adjust the heating or air conditioning. Close up the house until the floor is dry. Just opening a door can create a draft pulling dust into your wet finish.

Cure Time

Follow the directions on the urethane container for time to allow for complete drying. Many product containers tell you that they are highly cured in a certain period of time, but you should also take into consideration the overall climate at the time of coating - humidity level, temperature, direct sunlight, and other elements that could effect the dry time. Be careful to allow adequate drying time before you walk on the floor.

Screen Before Final

It's a good idea to lightly screen your floor prior to the application of the final coat. Screening is done using the same buffer that you used prior to staining. The screen most commonly used at this stage is 180 grit. It is a round pad that will lightly rough up the first coat of urethane to assure that the final coat will adhere correctly.

Vacuum, Then Vacuum Again

Screening will create a light layer of dust on the floor. Remember, even the smallest amount of dust on the floor will collect on your application pad during the urethane coat and become debris in the finish. Vacuum your floor after this final screening.

We also recommend that you dust yourself off completely, remove your hat and any articles of clothing that have dust on them. Remove your shoes and vacuum one more time.

The Final Coat

Check your applicator pads to be certain there is no debris stuck in the lambs wool or roller pad.

As you work in the final coat put good light on your project areas so you can catch any overlaps or debris.

Look As You Go

A good motto for all steps of coating is "Take A 2nd Look." It takes only a moment to pause and look carefully for any flaws in the floor's appearance.

And out the Door

Having placed all of your tools, vacuum, containers, clothing and shoes at an exit, or preferably in the garage, work your way to the exit door.

A final consideration for a good finish would be to place tape or a towel at the base of your exit door to assure that no air leaks under the door and deposits dust here. A strip of painters tape also works well.

If other members of your family are out, and you're not sure when they might come home, don't take a chance. Run a strip of tape across all access doors so they will know not to open a door and the newly finished floors are off limits for a time.

Coating the Quarter Round

Before you close your containers, organize your equipment and tools, you may want to put another coat on your quarter round or any other trim that you will be resetting.

✓ Finishing Checklist

❏ Polyurethane

❏ Water-based urethane

❏ Applicators needed

❏ Exit plan

❏ Close windows and doors

❏ Shut down heat or air

❏ Vacuum

❏ First coat

❏ Cure time to allow

❏ Screen before final coat

❏ Double vacuum

❏ Check applicator for debris

❏ Final coat

❏ Take a second look

❏ Coat quarter round and trim

Notes: _____

_____

_____

_____

_____

_____

_____

_____

_____

_____

_____

_____

_____

_____

_____

Chapter 10

Resetting the Trim

Resetting the Base and Installing Quarter Round

Installing your new hardwood flooring is an excellent time to clean up the baseboards in the project area. It will never be easier to work with it then it is now. A fresh coat of paint or a new coat of stain and urethane will help to give the entire floor area a new and fresh look.

When resetting the baseboard, which has been numbered for its designated place on the wall, use your compressor and finish nailer. It is good to double-check your compressor settings to be sure the finish nailer lightly counter-sinks the nail, but doesn't drive it too deep into the baseboard. Most painted baseboard is pine and very soft, so it is possible to drive the nail all the way through the board.

Be sure you press the base all the way down on the floor and all the way up against the wall before nailing. Shoot the nails into the upper half of the baseboard and into a stud if possible.

Using the same finish nailer, shoot the quarter round in under cabinets and other areas that may need to have the edge of the flooring covered.

Caulking

A good tip to remember when you get ready to caulk is in how you cut the end of your caulking tube. It is common to just cut the end of the tube off anywhere to open it up for the caulk to squeeze out. But there is a better way to do that for this project. Cut very near to the end of the tube nozzle (there are normally cut lines indicated on the plastic nozzle). Cut at an angle from the tip in. This is very important when you get to the phase of running a caulk bead across the top of the baseboard.

Now wet a household sponge, wring it out, and with your finger dab caulking (a color to match the wood finish) into the counter-sunk nail

Run the caulking bead along the top of the baseboard using a very small opening on the end of the caulk tube.

Wet your finger then run it very lightly along the bead of caulk giving a finished look to the baseboard.

holes along the baseboard and/or quarter round. Lightly wipe the wet sponge across those areas to even out the caulk to a smooth look. As the caulk dries it may shrink slightly and leave a small dimple. This will become less noticeable as you reset the rooms with furniture, throw rugs, and items that draw attention away from the tiny imperfections in normal floors and trim.

Your final caulking step is now to run a very thin bead of caulk along the top of the baseboard to conceal the small crack line between the baseboard and the wall. This will give a finished look to your project.

Run the caulking bead a few feet in front of you or the complete length of that wall area. After you have run the small bead wet your finger slightly on the sponge and lightly run your finger along the length of the bead. This will even out the line of caulk, giving a smooth transition from baseboard to wall. If the caulk builds up against your finger wipe it on a rag and continue, going back over the line a second time. If it spreads beyond the bead line on to the baseboard or wall use the sponge to wipe it clean. Having a sink or bucket of water handy can be helpful to keep the sponge clean and moist.

The Final Walk Through

Before calling your project complete we recommend you do a final walk through. Before you begin moving furniture, appliances, and other items back onto the floor, it is good to take a second look.

Be aware however, small dust specs will be in the floor under the urethane. Some of these are so near the surface they will walk off over time and wear. Do not try to sand, screen, or rub these specs. Sometimes very small pieces of debris can be scratched off with your fingernail. Scraping or abrasive pads risk marring the surface and leaving you with a noticeable blemish in the flooring.

It may seem reasonable to brush some urethane to blend in a spot, but efforts now to help a dry spot or blemish, can leave a new spot that will appear like a water puddle when it dries.

Moving Back in - Very Carefully

Allow plenty of time for the floor to cure before moving furniture and appliances back into the rooms. Although most urethanes will cure up to 85 percent within a few hours, that final percentage of cure should be allowed before setting heavy items on the finish, especially items with a great deal of weight on a small leg or wheel. Setting a refrigerator down in front of it's permanent space and then rolling it back into that space can leave roll marks or scratches in your new finish.

Golf spikes and athletic cleats can leave marks, indentations, and scratches on your hardwood floors. Be careful that high heeled shoes are in good repair where the heel contacts the floor. Measured in pounds per square inch (psi), a car has a load of 28-30 psi, an elephant 50-100 psi, and a 125 pound woman with high heels 2,000 psi!

Throw rugs in entries, in front of the sink, refrigerator, and stove top are essentials to keeping your finish strong and durable. It is important to consider UV rays and their effect on your wood and finishes. If your rear entry door from a deck or patio is all glass and gets direct afternoon sun, it is important that you move, or roll up the throw rug in front of that door regularly so the sunlight that will bleach that area will bleach evenly and not create different shades of flooring under the throw rug and around that area.

✓ Resetting Checklist

❑ Touch up baseboard

❑ Install baseboard

❑ Install quarter round

❑ Wet a sponge

❑ Caulk nail holes

❑ Caulk bead along top

❑ Final walk through

❑ Throw rugs

Notes: _____

_____

_____

_____

_____

_____

_____

_____

Chapter
11

The Final Touch

A Quality Check on Finish

As you look over your work giving it a final check be aware that according to National Wood Flooring Association standards, a hardwood floor should only be inspected from a standing position. To quote from the website of the NWFA:

> *Keep in mind that no two floor boards will be identical. Variations in appearance are completely normal. As your floor ages, some color change can occur. This also is normal, but can be minimized by limiting exposure to direct sunlight, and periodically moving furniture and rugs. Cracks are normal as well, and will appear and disappear between floor boards during seasons of high and low humidity. Generally, anything less than the width of a dime is considered normal, and will correct itself as seasons change. Flooring inspectors recommend inspecting the floor from a standing position in normal lighting to identify irregularities.*

As beautiful as your new hardwood flooring can be, it is still a floor. It is to be admired of course, but it is also meant to be walked on, spilled on and dropped on.

Felt Pads

Always put felt pads on the bottom of chair and table legs. Most hardware stores sell both the nail in and stick-on types of pads.

It is also a good idea to occasionally turn the chairs over and, using an old toothbrush, lightly brush any dust and dirt particles that may be embedded in the pads. Chair legs carry a good deal of weight on them and the smallest grime can eventually cause surface scratching on your hardwood finish.

Throw Rugs

Again throw rugs should go in heavy traffic areas, entries, in front of sink, stove, refrigerators and anywhere you stop, perform a task, then turn on your feet which can grind dirt particles into the finish and cause scratching.

Do not use throw rugs with rubber backing. This backing can cause a chemical discoloration in your finish. As hard as your floor finish is, it needs to breathe. Anything that seals off air can cause discoloring issues.

Cleaning Hardwood Floors

Do not use floor products on your hardwood floors that are not specifically recommended for hardwood floors and from known manufacturers. Using waxes, many oil-based cleaners, or vinyl and tile cleaners can cause floors to become slippery. These also dull their sheen and appearance over time. In addition, many of these products can prohibit a later maintenance coat from adhering correctly.

There are many good wood floor cleaning products on the market and available in most grocery and hardware stores.

We often hear that water and vinegar (four to one ratio) are good for cleaning hardwood floors. That is generally acceptable however be careful to not pour water directly onto the floor and if you use a mop make sure that mop is only a damp mop or sponge. Your floors will expand in the more humid months and contract in the dry winter months. This contraction will develop small cracking in parts of the floor's surface, which will allow excess water to run into those small cracks.

Hardwood floor cleaning products should help you keep a visible sheen on your floor and keep it from becoming too dull.

Humidifiers and Dehumidifiers

Due to the seasonal movement of hardwood flooring noted above, it will give your hardwood greater durability if you are able to keep a reasonably steady moisture level in your home. Keeping this movement to a minimum can be done using full system or room units. Like fine wood furniture, hardwood is easily effected by seasonal moisture changes.

Maintenance Coats

A maintenance coat, sometimes referred to as a "screen and recoat" is recommended periodically to keep the top coat of urethane finish fresh and protective of your wood floors.

How often you may need this coat is dependent upon the wear and tear your floor is exposed to. Tennis shoes carry pebbles, large dogs can be very hard on any type of floor, and active children with their toys, can cause surface wear over time.

As a rule of thumb, we would suggest that a period of from three-to-four years, on average, would be a good time to consider a maintenance coat for your hardwood floors.

A maintenance coat is like your final coat of urethane finish. A light screening to remove very light surface scratches, plus one new coat of urethane will renew the sheen on your flooring as well as add an additional new coat of protection for your hardwood.

If you do not apply a periodic maintenance coat, heavy traffic areas will not only wear down through the top coat of urethane, but through all urethane. This becomes apparent when your floor begins to have areas that have a very slight gray cast to them. This is dust that is now working into the wood grain itself where the urethane has been totally worn through. Only a full sand and refinish can cure that kind of problem.

Fillers and Cracking

Seasonal cracking is to be expected with hardwood flooring. As we have noted, up to the width of a dime can be expected in the dry winter months as your hardwood loses much of its moisture content and shrinks.

Although hardwood fillers, like those used during the original sand and finish, can be used to fill such cracks, it is advisable to let the wood move naturally during these periods. Filling those cracks in the dry months can result in the reverse problem in the humid months. As the hardwood takes on moisture again in spring and summer it expands, the small cracks close, and often the filler is pushed out and leaves you with filler edges along those cracks that can become even more noticeable.

Chapter
12

Additional Information

For additional information about hardwood flooring, species, grades, installation, finishing, and maintenance, you can go to the following websites:

Learn About Hardwood Flooring
       http://www.learnhardwoodflooring.com/

Hand-Crafted, Eco-Friendly Hardwood Flooring
       http://www.charleschristopherdesign.com/

National Wood Flooring Assocation (NWFA)
       http://www.woodfloors.org/consumer/index.aspx

National Oak Flooring Manufacturers Association (NOFMA)
       http://www.nofma.org/

Cleaning and Maintenance Products
       http://www.bonakemi.com/shop/products.asp